SUPER SPORTS
SNOW SPORTS

DAVID JEFFERIS

Chrysalis Children's Books

First published in Great Britain in
2001 by Chrysalis Children's Books
An imprint of Chrysalis Books
Group Plc
The Chrysalis Building,
Bramley Road,
London W10 6SP

Paperback edition first published in
2003
Copyright © David Jefferis 2001

Design and editorial production
Alpha Communications
Educational advisor Julie Stapleton
Picture research Kay Rowley

ISBN 1 84138 348 1 (hb)
ISBN 1 84138 765 7 (pb)

British Library Cataloguing in
Publication Data for this book is
available from the British Library.

Printed in China
10 9 8 7 6 5 4 3 2 1 (hb)
10 9 8 7 6 5 4 3 2   (pb)

Acknowledgements
We wish to thank the following
individuals and organizations for their
help and assistance and for supplying
material in their collections:
All Sport, Alpha Archive, Denis
Balibouse, Al Bello, Bombardier
Recreational Products, Erich Brenter,
Buzz Pictures, Shaun Botterill, Simon
Bruty, Ulrich Grill, Nick Groves, Mike
Hewitt, Jed Jacobsohn, Otto Kasper,
Lou Martin, Richard Martin, Darren
McNamara, Francois Portmann, Mike
Powell, Nick Rawcliffe, Red Bull
Communications Centre, Pascal
Rondeau, Nikolai Seavey, Jamie
Squire, Stock Shot, Vandystadt
Agency, Yamaha Motor Co, Zoom
Agency

Diagrams by Gavin Page

▲ Snowmobiles are
used for all sorts of
transportation in
snowy countries.
Snowmobile racing
is also popular.

Contents

 Look out for the Super Sports symbol
Look for the skier silhouette in boxes like this.
Here you will find extra snow sport facts, stories
and useful tips for beginners.

World of snow sports

There are many different snow sports. They are lots of fun to do and a great way to stay fit.

▲ Snowboards are almost as popular as skis at some resorts.

For most snow sports you will need skis of one shape or another to help you glide easily across the snow.

Whizzing down mountains is called alpine, or downhill, skiing. Nordic, or cross-country, skiing is just like walking, but on skis. It is slower than downhill skiing, but it's hard work, so cross-country skiers need lots of energy.

▼ Cross-country skiing is like walking on skis.

▶ Huskies are bred as working dogs in cold countries. They can also be used for sled races.

▲ Ski poles help skiers balance and turn. Goggles protect the eyes from glare.

▶ In most resorts, skiers reach the ski slopes by riding in chair lifts like the ones shown here, or in cable cars.

Downhill and slalom

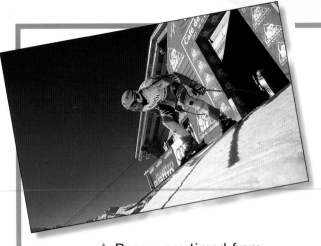

▲ Racers are timed from the moment they leave the starting gate.

Downhill racing is a very fast ski event over a long course. Slaloms are races in which skiers twist and turn along a winding downhill course.

▼ Great strength is needed to keep control in the turns of a slalom course.

Downhill skiers can reach speeds of 100 km/h or more, while racing down a wide, sweeping course. The course is marked by pairs of poles, called gates. Downhill racers use curved poles, which fit around their bodies, and they must wear safety helmets.

▲ Downhill racing slopes are wide and open, allowing skiers to reach high speeds without the risk of hitting an obstacle.

In slalom races, skiers race down a bendy course, zig-zagging between gates as they go. Skiers need to be skilled at making turns as fast and as tight as possible.

 Snow speak

Snow sports have their own special words. Here are some of them:

Binding   Safety fitting that joins a ski boot to a ski or snowboard.
Edge   Metal strip along each side of a ski. Gives grip in turns.
Fall line Route straight down the steepest part of a ski slope.
Piste   Area set out for skiers, with smoothed and cleared snow.
Schuss   Skiing downhill, with skis parallel to each other.
Traverse Skiing across the fall line, rather than straight down.

Cross-country skiing

Cross-country ski courses include sections that are on the flat, as well as uphills and downhills. Skiers use special skis that are longer than Alpine skis.

▲ Biathlon races combine a tough cross-country course with target shooting.

To glide smoothly along, cross-country skiers either slide on their skis and push forward with their poles, or use a skating movement. Races cover various distances, from short sprint events to long marathons.

Cross-country ski routes are often prepared using machines that crush flattened paths through the snow.

► Cross-country racing is very hard work on flat and uphill sections.

Uphill climb by herringbone

A cross-country ski has a special surface on the bottom to give grip when going up gentle slopes.

On gentle hill climbs, skiers use a 'herringbone' movement. The skis are angled into a v-shape so the edges push into the snow for extra grip.

Skiers have to side-step up steep hills, which is much slower.

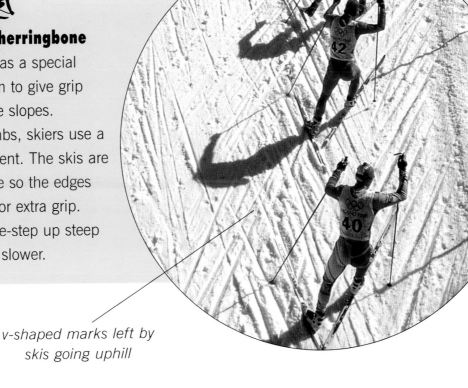

v-shaped marks left by skis going uphill

▲ A cross-country racer keeps going as the weather closes in for a big snowstorm.

Freestyle stunts

Freestyle stunts are acrobatics on skis. In the most spectacular stunts, called aerials, skiers launch into the air off a short ramp called a kicker.

Aerial stunts involve amazing acrobatics, such as side-twists, somersaults and spins. In competitions, judges give points for a good take off and landing, as well as for skill in the mid-air stunts.

Another freestyle event is acroski, which is like a ski-ballet. Skiers perform a jumping, spinning dance routine in time to music.

Mogul freestylers ski down a slope packed with mounds of snow called moguls. Skiers jump off the moguls and are scored on how well they turn and jump, as well as how fast they go.

◀ Once airborne, an aerial freestyler may do one, two or even three somersaults.

Smoothing the piste

At big resorts, the pistes are prepared every night ready for skiing next day.

One of the most important tools is a piste-maker, like the machine shown here. The driver scoops snow neatly into place with a big snowplough.

Piste-makers cannot tackle the steepest slopes, and here snow may form mounds, or moguls – perfect for mogul freestylers.

wide tracks give the piste-maker grip on most slopes

▼ A freestyler spins round and round in a movement called the helicopter.

Ski jump

Ski jumping is a sport for the brave. Jumpers ski down a steep ramp called the in-run, then shoot into the air for a distance of 70 metres or more, before landing again.

▲ Ski-jump ramps at dawn, ready for an early start to the day's events.

▲ Points are awarded for style as well as distance in the air. This skier holds his body and skis parallel to one another, but holding the front tips apart in a v-shape is popular too.

Ski jumpers try to stay airborne as long as possible. But to get high scores in competitions they must also keep their legs, skis and body under control.

Landings are made between two lines called the norm and table points. It's dangerous to go much further as there may not be room to stop safely.

Jump skis are based on cross-country skis, but are longer, wider and heavier. Grooves underneath the skis help to give the skier control in flight.

▲ Jumpers go down the in-run crouched low to build up speed.

Top marks for a stylish jump

Ski jumpers lose points for faults on take off, flight and landing. If a jumper touches the snow with a hand when landing, for example, that counts as a fault. Most ski-jumps are between 70m and 120m. Ski-flying is another event, which is scored only on the distance flown.

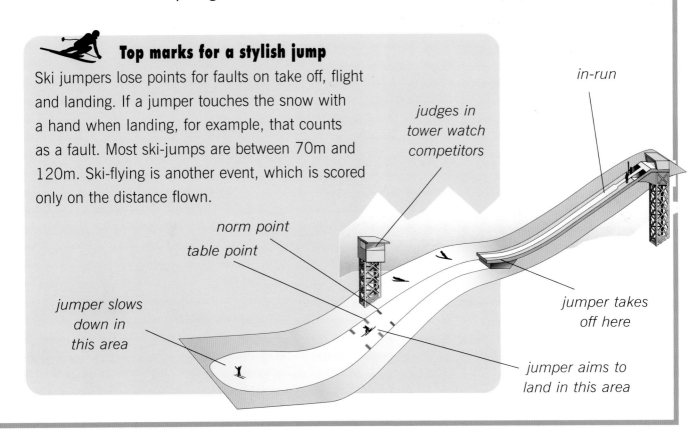

in-run

judges in tower watch competitors

norm point

table point

jumper takes off here

jumper slows down in this area

jumper aims to land in this area

Snowboards

▲ Beginners start on gentle nursery slopes.

Snowboarders use a wide, surfboard-shaped ski instead of a pair of long, narrow skis. Snowboards are great for doing all sorts of aerial stunts.

Boarders stand sideways with their boots locked on to the board. They use their body and arms to help keep their balance.
Steering a board is like using the rudder on a boat. The board is turned to the left or right when the boarder pushes with the toes or heel of his back foot.
There are downhill and freestyle events for snowboards, and many resorts have pistes set aside for these.

◄ This snowboarder is a 'regular' – he rides with his left foot forward. Some boarders lead with the right foot, and are known as 'goofies'.

riders of all shapes and sizes can find a board to fit

14

▼ Snowboards are high-fashion items and come in a great variety of different colours and patterns.

▲ Many snowboarders learn skills such as 'hanging air', shown here. It's like a snow version of skateboarding.

Building a snowboard

Boards and skis look simple enough, but designing them is a skilled job. They are made of layers of material, joined together to make a strong sandwich.

The centre, or core, is usually made of many thin layers of wood – often ash or birch. Other materials surround the core to finish off the board's construction.

A good board is strong, but has spring in it to make jumps and turns easier.

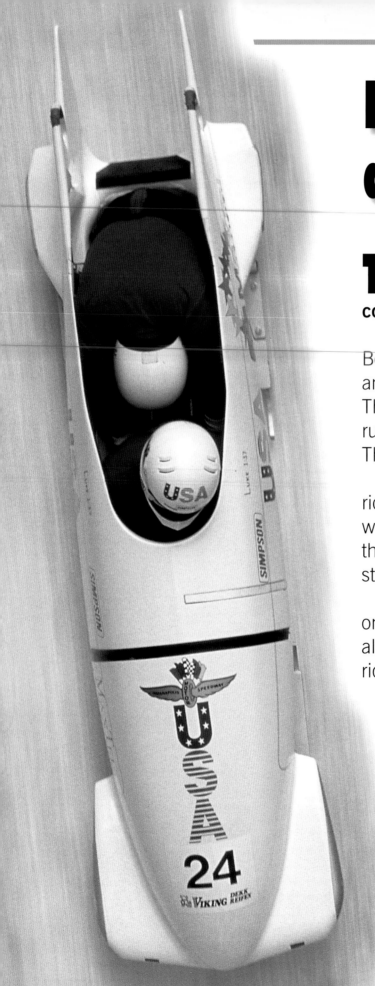

Bobsleigh and luge

These are toboggans built for racing. They hurtle down a smooth, icy course at very high speeds.

Bobsleighs race, one at a time, down an icy run, at speeds of over 100 km/h. The crew push the bobsleigh down the run to build up speed before leaping in. They wear spiked shoes to grip the ice.

Speeding down the run, the front rider steers and the person at the back works the brakes. In a four-person bob, the two middle crew members help to steady the bob as it goes round corners.

A luge is like a toboggan. Riders lie on their backs during a race. There are also two-place luges, in which one rider lies on top of the other!

◀ A two-person team crouches behind the bodywork of a bobsleigh. The driver steers. The rear person puts on the brakes when they are needed.

▲ A team runs hard to launch a bobsleigh. The front two crew members push the bob with handles that fold neatly away during the race.

Losing control at over 100 km/h

A luge is little more than a plastic and metal seat, built to slide down a smooth, icy track, called a run.

Riders lie back on the luge and go down the run feet-first. They hang on to a strap and steer by leaning from side to side. Crashes happen regularly, but luckily serious injuries are rare.

a helmet is essential in case of a crash

Snowmobiles

▲ Riders lean into corners to stay upright. Wide front skis help keep the snowmobile level.

Snowmobiles speed across the snow like motor bikes. The front skis are used for steering and an engine provides the power.

The first snowmobiles were made in 1959 as a speedy way to travel in snowy countries.

Modern snowmobiles can shoot across the snow at speeds of 100 km/h or more. They have skis at the front for steering and a track whizzing round under the seat which pushes them forward.

Today, snowmobile racing is a popular snow sport with dozens of competitions taking place throughout the winter months.

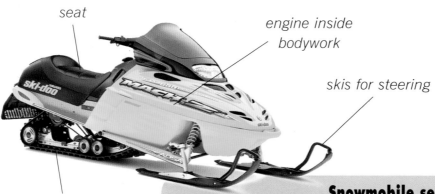

seat

engine inside bodywork

skis for steering

track is used instead of wheels

Snowmobile secrets

The snowmobile's success lies in its skis and wide rubber drive track. The track grips the snow much better than wheels and sends the snowmobile shooting forward. The skis let the driver steer the machine almost anywhere, without it sinking into the snow. The skis are turned with the handlebars.

Snowmobiles are used for all sorts of jobs. For example, polar explorers use them for towing supplies.

► Racing snowmobiles need thorough checking. The rear track can be fitted with metal spikes for extra grip.

spiked rubber track

▼ Only an expert rider can perform high-speed stunts like this safely.

plastic screen keeps cold wind off rider's chest

Snow explorers

Making trips into distant mountain areas is a great idea for people who want more than a few days skiing in a resort area.

Careful planning is essential for people who ski in high mountains. If a storm blows up suddenly, it may be some time before help arrives.

It's possible to be snowed in for several days, so emergency food rations are necessary, as is a tough, stormproof tent that's quick to put up.

▲ Snowshoes let walkers travel in soft snow. They used to be made of wood and rope. New designs are in metal and plastic.

◀ Backpacks are loaded carefully for good balance on the move.

A week in the wild

An exciting adventure for ski explorers is to be flown into a distant mountain area by plane or helicopter.

The days are spent skiing, using maps to stay on course. The nights are spent in lightweight tents which keep out the cold. After a week in the snow, the explorers are picked up and flown home.

lightweight tent folds flat and packs into a small bag

▶ The air may be cold, but skiing cross-country can be hot work, especially uphill. There may be snowstorms, so using good survival gear is very important.

Dogsled races

husky

wolf

In Alaska, husky dogs were once used as working dogs to carry freight and mail. Today, huskies also go racing!

The most famous husky race is the Iditerod, which is held in Alaska every March. It is a long race, nearly 1700 km. Teams of 12-18 dogs normally complete the race in about ten days. Each dog team has a person called a musher in charge.

The race's rules are strict, especially where the dogs are concerned. Each dog is checked for good health before and during the race.

▲ The ancestor of the husky is the wolf. Both animals can survive easily in the cold.

▶ Teams of huskies are harnessed together with a lead dog at the front.

What's in a name?

The Iditerod gets its name from a word used by native Americans of the Athabasca tribe. It means 'the distant place' and was first used to describe inland hunting grounds.

The dog-team drivers are known as mushers, a term that comes from the French for walking, *marcher*. In the nineteenth and early twentieth centuries, Alaskans described almost any travel over snow as mushing.

▲ A team of huskies is expensive to feed. These dogs earn their keep between races by hauling tourists on sightseeing rides.

harnesses join the huskies to the sled

New ideas

New snow equipment is being developed all the time. Lightweight skis make skiing easier and safer, and modern fabrics help to make lighter, warmer clothing.

▲ The snowbone is a board for beginners. Riders hold the handle and can jump off if they make a mistake.

New equipment makes learning to ski easier for beginners. For example, short skis are lighter than normal ones and easier to use. Once you have learned the basics, it isn't difficult to progress to full-size skis.

Ski safety is very important and wearing a helmet is becoming popular, especially for children.

As ski equipment improves, competition skiers are able to set new records for speed.

▼ Heli-skiing allows skiers to reach distant peaks, but it is an expensive sport.

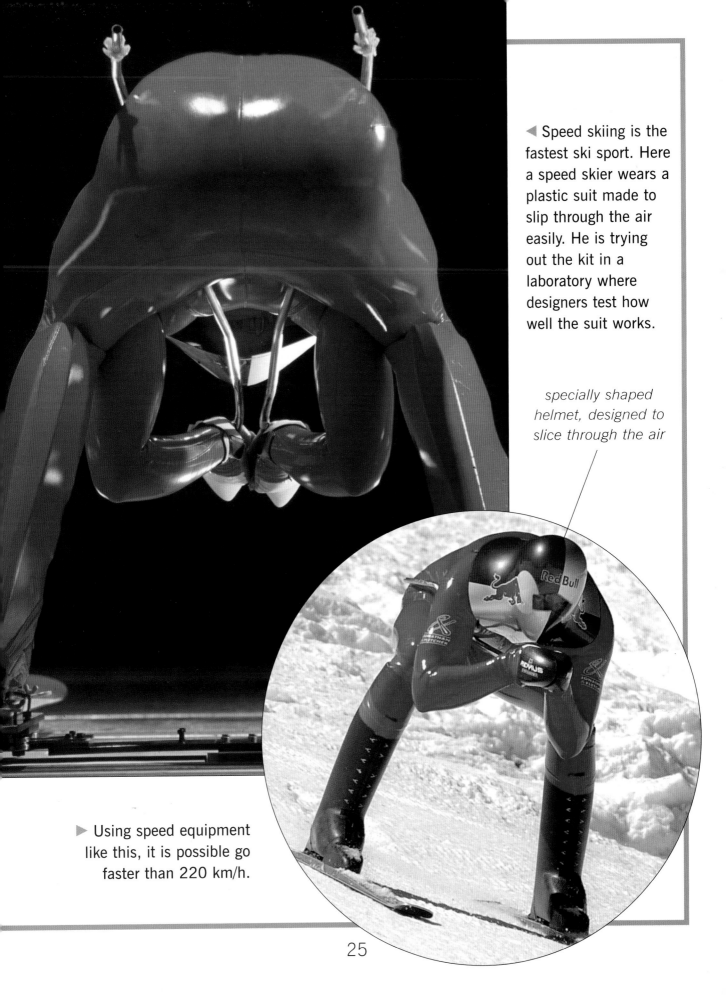

◀ Speed skiing is the fastest ski sport. Here a speed skier wears a plastic suit made to slip through the air easily. He is trying out the kit in a laboratory where designers test how well the suit works.

specially shaped helmet, designed to slice through the air

▶ Using speed equipment like this, it is possible go faster than 220 km/h.

▲ A ski-bob rider at speed.

Snow sport facts

Here are some facts and stories from the world of snow sports.

The first skiers

Skiing started to be popular only about 120 years ago. But skis have been used in some places for much longer.

The oldest ski in the world was found in Sweden. It is thought to be about 4500 years old. It is made of pine, and has a slot for a foot to fit in, with holes for bindings. There are also rock carvings showing ski-hunters, which may be even older.

Hillside ski jumps

Ski sports began in Norway, when Sondre Norheim started ski jumping in the 1840s. He was the first skier to jump down steep hillsides.

Norheim also improved ski equipment, which helped him win prizes in an 1868 ski competition.

Speedy luge...

The top speed for a luge run is held by a Norwegian, Asle Strand. In 1982 he hurtled downhill at over 137 km/h.

... but faster ski-bob

Ski-bobs are like bicycles on skis. Riders use mini-skis clipped to their boots to help them balance when cornering. But ski-bobs can go much faster than the average bike with wheels. In 1999 a Swiss ski-bob rider achieved a speed of 173 km/h!

◀ Training for cross-country events is hard work. Competitors need to be very fit.

◀ A luge racer starts a run with a mighty heave at the start gate.

Hero of the snow

The Iditerod dogsled race in Alaska takes place every year to honour the memory of a husky dog called Balto.

In 1925, Balto led a dog-team taking medicine to the town of Nome, where there was an outbreak of the disease diphtheria.

The weather was terrible, with blinding snow storms, very high winds and icy-cold temperatures.

The 1085km route was covered by a number of husky relay teams. Balto led the final team into Nome, after an 85km run through the snow.

Finland's mega-race

The world's biggest ski race is held in Finland each year, and thousands of people take part. The cross-country course is 75 km long. One year 13 226 competitors entered! Most people completed the course, with only 317 not making it to the finish line.

Cresta run

The Cresta run, at St Moritz in Switzerland, is the home of bobsleigh racing. The fastest bob has covered the 1212m course in just 50.09 seconds.

One-day endurance

Finland comes tops for many snow-sports events, including tough tests such as skiing non-stop for 24 hours. In 1988, Seppo-Juhani Savolainen covered 415.5 km in the exactly timed event – which works out to an average speed of more than 17 km/h.

front runners turn to steer   *engine*   *propeller at back*

▶ In 1922, 15-year-old Canadian Joseph-Armand Bombardier built an early type of snowmobile. His 'snow-sleigh' (right) was powered by a propeller.

Later on, in 1959, Bombardier's company launched the modern-style snowmobile, which was called a Ski-Doo.

Snow sport words

▲ Freestyle aerial.

Here are some technical terms used in this book.

alpine skiing
Alpine, or downhill, is the name for skiing down mountains. The other type of skiing is cross-country, or nordic.

biathlon
A competition containing two activities. In skiing events, a biathlon may combine cross-country with target shooting.

bindings
Clips that join boots to skis or snowboards. Bindings release if a skier falls over, to avoid breaking a leg or ankle.

chair lift
A system of chairs that carry skiers up mountains. The chairs hang from a cable that moves between metal pylons.

▶ Bindings join boots to skis.

edge
The metal sides of a ski. They are tougher than the rest of the ski, and take the strain of cornering by carving into the snow or ice.

fall line
A route leading straight down the steepest part of a slope. Crossing the fall line from side to side is called traversing.

freestyle
Acrobatics on skis or on a snowboard. There are three types of freestyle event: aerial, acroski and mogul.

gate
A pair of marker poles used in ski racing. There is also a starting gate.

heli-skiing
Using a helicopter to give skiers a lift up to a distant or very high snow slope.

herringbone
A method of climbing up a gentle slope on skis. Skis are put into a v-shape so the skier can press back into the snow to get up the hill.

mogul
A mound of snow created by skiers turning on a steep slope. Lots of them in one area is called a mogul field.

boots clipped into bindings at toes and heels

28

musher
The driver in charge of a dogsled team. The term comes from the French word for walking, *marcher*.

nordic skiing
See alpine skiing.

norm point
The first of three landing points on a ski-jump slope. A jumper aims to land at the table point. The critical point is the last point at which there is room to stop safely.

nursery slope
Gently sloping area at a ski resort, suitable for beginners.

parallel ski
Skiing with skis in line with each other.

piste
A ski area that is specially prepared for skiers.

poles
Sticks used by skiers to help with balance, especially when turning sharply.

▲ Skiers use poles to help balance during downhills and slaloms.

run
A ski or snowboard course, or the icy slope of a bobsleigh or luge course.

schuss
A straight-line ski course, often down a fall line.

slalom
A downhill ski race which weaves through marker gates. Also describes a zigzag downhill course.

snowshoe
An extra-large outer shoe, made to spread the weight of a walker on the snow.

◄ Cable cars do a similar job to chair lifts. Skiers ride up the mountain in small cabins.

Snow science

There is lots to learn about snow and the science behind snow sports.

◀ Skis slide easily because they have slippery bottoms, or soles. These are usually made of plastic, but they may need waxing to keep them smooth.

front ends of skis are called tips

▲ Snowboards also need to be smooth.

Why do skis need to be smooth?

Smooth skis slide much more easily on snow, which allows a skier to go faster. This experiment shows you the difference between a rough surface and a smooth surface.

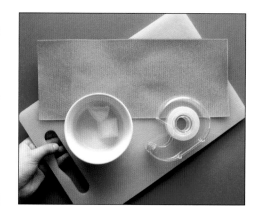

1 You need two ice cubes, a sheet of sandpaper, a kitchen cutting board and some tape.

2 Lay the sandpaper on one side of the board. Tape it down at each end to keep it in place.

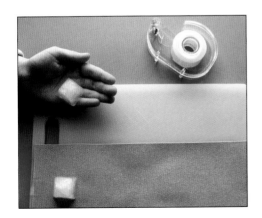

Powder snow forms when the temperature is well below freezing.

Where does snow come from?

Snow falls as flakes, each one made up of ice crystals. The ice crystals come in different shapes, such as needles and hexagons. They are formed from the water vapour inside clouds. All snowflakes have a six-sided shape, but each flake's pattern is slightly different.

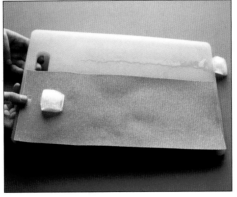

Snowflakes come in many shapes, but all have six sides. There are many different sorts of snow, from fine, dry powder to heavy, wet slush.

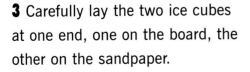

3 Carefully lay the two ice cubes at one end, one on the board, the other on the sandpaper.

4 Gently lift the board to make a slope. See which cube whizzes to the bottom of the slope first.

Index